Binturongs

Victoria Blakemore

vblakemore.author@gmail.com

Copyright info/picture credits

Cover, Dasha Petrenko/AdobeStock; Page 3, phichak/AdobeStock; Page 5, phichak/AdobeStock; Page 7, coffeemill/AdobeStock; Page 9, bouybin/Adobestock; Pages 10-11, Fotos 593/AdobeStock; Page 13, Evgenia Silaeva/AdobeStock; Page 15, noppharat/AdobeStock; Page 17, Prapassorn/AdobeStock; Page 19, Andrea Izzotti/AdobeStock; Page 21, ake/AdobeStock; Page 23; tope007/AdobeStock; Page 25, Sergey Skleznev/AdobeStock; Page 27, MemoryCatcher/Pixabay; Page 29, kajornyot/AdobeStock; Page 31, seraphic06/AdobeStock; Page 33, Dasha Petrenko/AdobeStock

Table of Contents

What Are Binturongs?

Binturongs are mammals

that are often called

"bearcats."

This is because they have

paws and claws like a bear,

and a cat-like face. Their

whiskers are also like a cat's

whiskers.

Size

The body of an adult
binturong is usually between
two and three feet long.
Their tail can be up to three
feet long.

Most adult binturongs weigh
between thirty and fifty
pounds.

Female binturongs are
usually larger and heavier
than male binturongs.

Physical Characteristics

Binturongs have long, shaggy fur which helps to keep them dry. They groom their fur like a cat, licking and biting it to keep it clean.

A binturong's tail is **prehensile** like a monkey's tail. It can curl and wrap around branches.

It can also help binturongs

balance as they move

through the trees.

Habitat

Binturongs live in the rainforest, where it is warm and there are lots of tall trees.

Binturongs usually stay up high in the trees. They do not come down to the ground very often. They are rarely seen by people in the wild.

Range

Binturongs are only found in the rainforests of South Asia.

They are found in countries

such as India, Thailand, China,

and Indonesia.

Diet

Binturongs are listed as **carnivores**. They eat mainly meat. They also sometimes eat fruit.

Their diet is made up of fish, insects, birds, fruit, and small mammals like rats.

Binturongs spend a lot of time eating. They can eat their own weight in food everyday.

Binturongs catch their prey with their long, sharp claws. They keep their claws sharp by scratching tree branches, like cats do with scratching posts.

Their claws also help them to climb trees to look for food.

Binturongs get much of their water from the food they eat. They do still need to drink water sometimes.

Communication

Binturongs use sound and scent to communicate. They make sounds like snorts, howls, wails, and growls.

They have a scent gland under their tail. It lets them leave their scent on tree branches. The scent tells other animals that a binturong lives there.

Binturongs have a very **unique**

scent. They smell like buttered

popcorn!

Movement

Binturongs have special ankles that can turn and bend. This lets them climb down tree trunks head first.

Binturongs walk on flat feet like bears do. They usually walk slowly when they are on the ground.

Binturongs spend most of their time in trees. They are able to move quickly across branches.

Staying Cool

Binturongs have a very thick coat of fur. This can be a problem for them when it gets too hot. They can **overheat**.

Binturongs cannot sweat, so they need to **release** their extra heat another way. They do this through panting.

When it gets hot, binturongs rest

in the shade and pant to cool

down.

Binturong Life

Binturongs are usually **solitary**. They prefer to spend most of their time alone. The only time they are seen is groups is when the cubs are with their mother.

Binturongs may be active during the day or at night.

Binturongs like to sleep and rest in the sun. They lie across branches in the sunlight.

Binturong Cubs

Binturongs have a **litter** of between 1 and 6 babies. Their babies are called cubs.

Cubs are born blind with very thin fur. Their eyes open after a few days. Their fur will become thicker as they get older.

Cubs stay with their mothers

until they are able to feed

themselves.

Helping the Rainforest

Binturongs have a special way they help the rainforest. The seeds from fruits that they eat are not fully broken down in their stomach.

The seeds are **dispersed** to different parts of the rainforest through the binturong's waste.

Strangler figs often grow from seeds that are spread by binturongs.

Population

Binturongs are listed as **vulnerable**. Their populations have been **decreasing**. If this continues, they may soon be **endangered**.

The binturong is almost **extinct** in parts of China and Vietnam.

In the wild, binturongs often live

between ten and fifteen years.

Binturongs in Danger

The biggest threat that binturongs face comes from people. Their habitats are being destroyed to make space for roads and buildings.

Binturongs are also caught to be pets or sent to zoos. Some **cultures** use parts of binturongs to make medicine.

Helping Binturongs

There are groups that are trying to help binturongs. They are working to protect the binturong's habitat from being destroyed.

They are also trying to get laws passed to protect binturongs from being caught by people.

Glossary

Carnivore: an animal that eats mostly meat

Decreasing: getting smaller

Dispersed: spread

Endangered: at risk of becoming extinct

Extinct: no more left

Litter: a group of animals born at the same time

Overheat: get too hot

Prehensile: able to hold onto

things

Release: to let go of

Solitary: living alone

Unique: different, special

Vulnerable: an animal that is

likely to become endangered

About the Author

Victoria Blakemore is a first grade

teacher in Southwest Florida with a

passion for reading.

You can visit her at

www.elementaryexplorers.com

Also in This Series

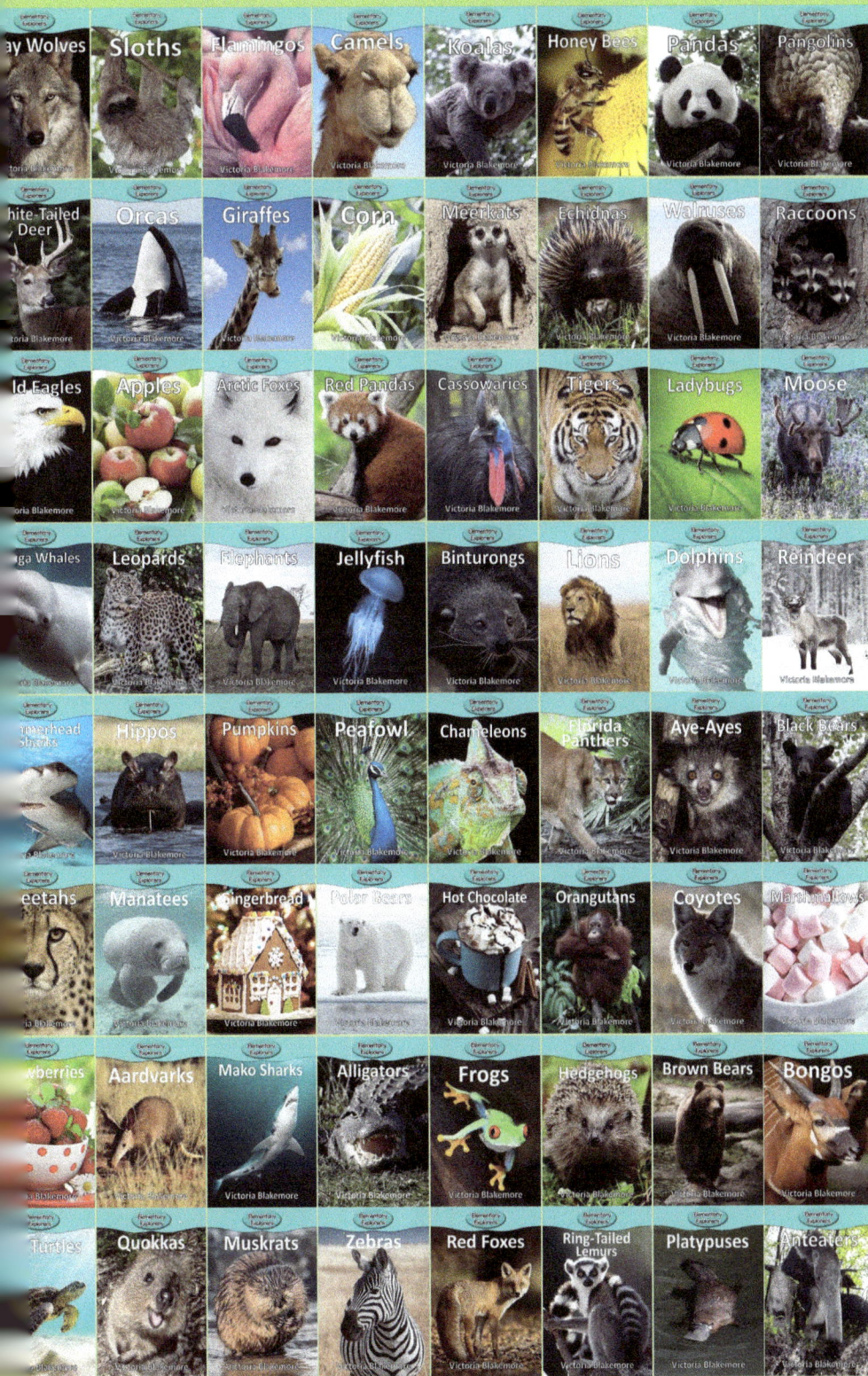

Gray Wolves	Sloths	Flamingos	Camels	Koalas	Honey Bees	Pandas	Pangolins
White-Tailed Deer	Orcas	Giraffes	Corn	Meerkats	Echidnas	Walruses	Raccoons
Bald Eagles	Apples	Arctic Foxes	Red Pandas	Cassowaries	Tigers	Ladybugs	Moose
Beluga Whales	Leopards	Elephants	Jellyfish	Binturongs	Lions	Dolphins	Reindeer
Hammerhead Sharks	Hippos	Pumpkins	Peafowl	Chameleons	Florida Panthers	Aye-Ayes	Black Bears
Cheetahs	Manatees	Gingerbread	Polar Bears	Hot Chocolate	Orangutans	Coyotes	Marshmallows
Strawberries	Aardvarks	Mako Sharks	Alligators	Frogs	Hedgehogs	Brown Bears	Bongos
Turtles	Quokkas	Muskrats	Zebras	Red Foxes	Ring-Tailed Lemurs	Platypuses	Anteaters

Also in This Series

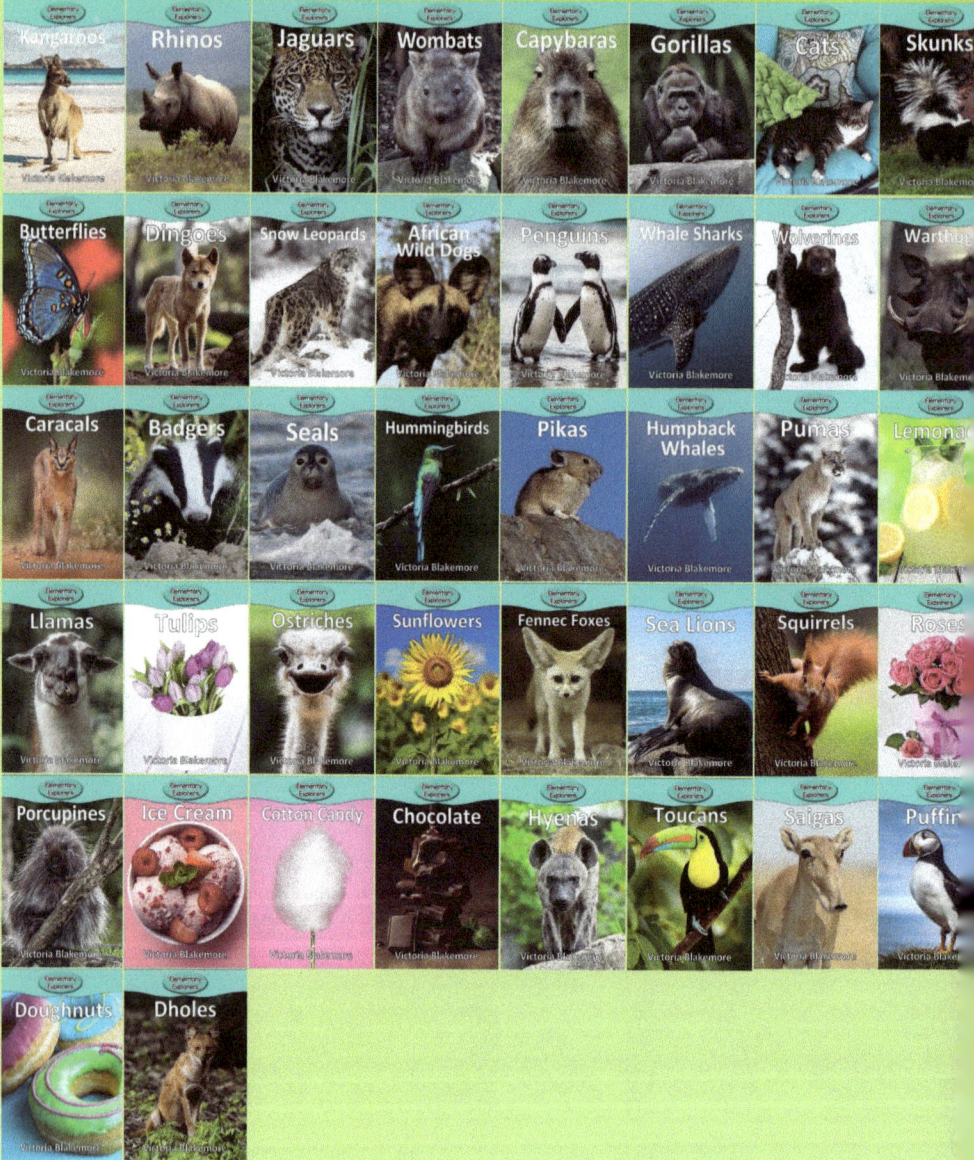

Kangaroos	Rhinos	Jaguars	Wombats	Capybaras	Gorillas	Cats	Skunks
Butterflies	Dingoes	Snow Leopards	African Wild Dogs	Penguins	Whale Sharks	Wolverines	Warthogs
Caracals	Badgers	Seals	Hummingbirds	Pikas	Humpback Whales	Pumas	Lemonade
Llamas	Tulips	Ostriches	Sunflowers	Fennec Foxes	Sea Lions	Squirrels	Roses
Porcupines	Ice Cream	Cotton Candy	Chocolate	Hyenas	Toucans	Saigas	Puffins
Doughnuts	Dholes						

www.ingramcontent.com/pod-product-compliance
Lightning Source LLC
Chambersburg PA
CBHW051250020426

42333CB00025B/3147